Fear

to

Courage

Kim Vastine
Paige Henderson
Sharon Kay Ball

The Freedom Series
Created by Michelle Borquez

AspirePress

Torrance, California

Fear to Courage

© Copyright 2013 God Crazy/Bella Publishing
Aspire Press, a division of Rose Publishing, Inc.
4733 Torrance Blvd., #259
Torrance, California 90503 USA

www.aspirepress.com
Register your book at www.aspirepress.com/register
Get inspiration via email, sign up at www.aspirepress.com

The views and opinions expressed in this book are those of the authors and do not necessarily express the views of Aspire Press, nor is this book intended to be a substitute for mental health treatment or professional counseling.

Scripture taken from the New American Standard Bible, © Copyright 1960, 1962, 1963, 1968, 1971, 1972, 1973, 1975, 1977, 1995 by The Lockman Foundation. Used by permission.

Printed in the United States.

Contents

The Authors

Kim Vastine was nearly crushed by the paralyzing fear, pain, and anger ingrained from a childhood full of unacknowledged abuse. She found her refuge and confidence in God, and then she founded Ambassador Alliance International (AAI), a ministry of justice and reconciliation for those who have no voice.

Paige Henderson is sought after nationally and internationally as a speaker who loves unlocking the passion in the hearts of women. Paige and her husband, Richard, founded Fellowship of the Sword Ministries [www.fellowshipofthesword.com].

Sharon Kay Ball is a licensed professional counselor and a mother to three children. In addition to her private practice, Sharon is a staff counselor at her church. Her own personal experience with suffering, the daily grind of single parenting, and counseling her clients has given Sharon tremendous compassion and insight for those dealing with life's tragedies and trials.

Chapter 1

Kim's Story

By Kim Vastine

"For you have been my help, and in the shadow of your wings I will sing for joy."
—Psalm 63:7

The pounding of an impatient fist knocking on the wooden frame of our front door sounded relentless. It was one of those beautiful California days that had a tantalizing combination of warm sunshine and a cool breeze from the nearby bay of the Pacific Ocean. My mother had left the front door wide open so that the outside air could be welcomed in through the locked, screen door.

"Hello, anyone home? Hello, Kim, are you here? The relentless knocking on the screen door jolted me out of my childhood afternoon reverie. Curiosity prompted me to skip from the patio through the house to see who was at the door. Upon reaching the front room, my eagerness was quickly replaced with a sickening panic as I recognized the figure of the man peering through the screen. He saw me, grinned from ear to ear, and his tone changed immediately to a sweet, syrupy drawl. "Kim, honey, how are you? Let me in, okay?"

Overwhelming feelings of dread grounded me to a frozen posture in the middle of the living room. Familiar fingers of fear began to tighten around my throat. I simply could not find my voice to utter a responsive word. My face felt hot and my stomach began to churn violently as the heat of shame surfaced. Sounding impatient now, Uncle Buck's voice grew stronger, "Kim, honey, what's wrong? Come on now, let me in. I brought you something."

Then I heard the familiar sound behind me of my feisty little grandmother running from the garage. I felt the angry energy in her ample, yet agile, body as she raced around me to the front door. She began loudly berating the man whose face held no expression. "How dare you show up at this house, you sucker! Get out of here *now* or I will call the police! Don't you ever show your face here again."

Uncle Buck stood there stunned. He quickly regained his composure, then looked past my grandmother at me. "Kim, did you tell our special secret? How could you do that? You promised me …"

When I was a child, "Uncle Buck" was a friendly, distant relative in the family who occasionally stopped by to visit. I enjoyed the special attention and compliments he handed out to me like candy. It seemed that he really saw me. So when Uncle Buck had stopped by one day when mama was at work and I was alone, I was happy to see a familiar face. When he came inside the house and took me to my parents' room to ask for a personal favor, I began to sense

I both admired and feared my abuser.

that something was wrong. But I was just a little girl—a good little girl. I could not tell an adult "no."

I hated what he made me do with him. Not just that time, but on other occasions too. Afterwards, he would give me the change in his pocket because I was such a "good girl." I asked him to stop, but he ignored my tearful pleas and said he just could not help it. I came to despise being a good girl, but I also craved approval and attention.

After Uncle Buck started visiting me, my grandmother moved in with our family. She was my best friend, and my siblings and I thought we were the luckiest kids to have her with us for a while. She was a retired nurse and took great care of our scratches and bumps with warm hugs and bandages. Her pies and cinnamon rolls were the talk of the family.

I was only seven years old, but I kept Uncle Buck's and my "secret." Like most children who are victims of abuse, I both admired and feared my abuser. I was ashamed and didn't want to get anyone in trouble. So when Grandma had demanded to know why I kept displaying signs of physical hurt and discomfort, I didn't admit a thing. She then marched me into the bedroom to see what was going on. It was obvious that I had been severely sexually abused. Terrified and confused, I confessed. I felt deep grief at exposing someone and was convinced it was my entire fault.

As a child, the agony and torment inside my body and mind were relentless. How could I have been so untrustworthy as to betray Uncle Buck? I had promised him I would never share "our little secret." After my initial confession, my father reported it to the local district attorney's office. I don't remember anyone ever asking me for full details about what occurred with Uncle Buck. As a young girl, and later as a young woman, I certainly never offered to talk about it. Rather, our family pretended it never happened, even later when a sexually transmitted disease attacked my body. As bad as it was physically, emotionally it was worse. The cancerous tentacles of the secret were not excised and they found fertile soil to flourish in my heart and soul.

Our family life was a contradiction. There were days when we looked fairly normal. Other days, well, it felt like we lived in hell. Mama took us to church every Sunday morning. We also went on Sunday, Tuesday and Thursday nights, and attended endless revival meetings. Seasonally, my dad would go with us. Early on I discovered that I loved to sing, and people seemed to enjoy listening. Congregational and solo singing at church gave me a voice. It was a way for my heart to be heard and accepted. I sang soulfully and passionately. Music was a healing gateway; my voice gave me value. I sensed the Lord actually heard me and loved my "song voice."

Music was a healing gateway.

I remember one special day in the tiny church prayer room when I poured out my plea for Jesus to come into my heart and save me. It was a wrenching, guttural cry for salvation and rescue on so many levels. That day, I felt his presence surround me in a way I had never known. A mountainous weight lifted off me, as wave after wave of his love washed over my spirit.

Soon, however, the weight returned. The preaching from the pulpit in my church produced an endless list of rules that qualified as sins. It was great training for me to become a judgmental "Pharisee" at a young age.

At night, sleep became elusive until I was sure I had repented of every possible sin I had committed that day. The need for approval became an idol in my life.

The need for approval became an idol in my life.

My father struggled to know how to show healthy love. He was filled with volcanic rage and a voice that wielded damaging words like a machete. Explosions occurred with little notice. It seemed that the most inconspicuous events or movement could set off a series of actions that would leave us three children and our mother cowering, sobbing, or desperately striving to seem invisible.

One day, my dad began screaming and angrily dragging my mother by the hair of her head. He yanked her out our front door and down the front lawn for all the neighbors to see. Another time he pinned her down on the bed, waving a knife near her throat and screaming that he was going to kill her. We kids sat terrified and helpless at the kitchen table, trying to see the tuna sandwiches on our lunch plates through a puddle of tears.

Dad found solace in the garage by hand carving wood into unique shapes to be used as paddles for our beatings. One time, my little sister and I watched in horror as he used heavy-duty rope to string up my brother by his arms to an old iron swing set with eight-foot poles. My father let him hang there as punishment for some wrongdoing. Any infraction called for punishment. If the garage light was left on, we would hear him scream our names to line up for the whippings until one of us confessed. We became great liars.

Dad came and went, and finally left home permanently, divorcing my mom when I was ten. A year later, we were given scholarships to attend our church school. Hopelessness filled me the day my brother and I were sent to the pastor's office to receive disciplinary swats for saying the forbidden slang word "wow." Bitter anger and fear silenced me as his swats hit their mark. We were in familiar territory. In my world, only men had power. God, whose love and acceptance I had felt so clearly in my little-girl cry for salvation, now seemed silent and still. My voice was silent, but my heart cried out for justice.

The abuse I received and witnessed throughout my early years left their mark through adolescence and long into adulthood. Did God really love me? Where was he when life was unfair? I buried these questions deep down in my heart and soul. I was good at pretending bad things weren't there. But anger, abuse, disappointment, unforgiveness and sadness won't stay buried forever. Like splinters under your skin, eventually they become infected, painfully working their way back to the surface. My emotional pain and anger stayed buried under a mask of service and striving—until the infection started leaking out into my "perfect Christian" life.

My identity was found in serving the church.

By the age of twenty-five, I had been married for six years and had a precious three-year-old daughter. I should have been on top of the world, but the internal need to be the perfect Christian, wife, mother, daughter, servant, and businesswoman was crushing me. My identity was found in serving the church rather than knowing my Redeemer, Jesus Christ. I wanted to know love, but crossing over a canyon of insignificance and anger, which manifested itself in road rage and general impatience with the world, only increased the unrelenting sadness.

The turning point began the day I drove home from work screaming and weeping profusely. "God, this anger and pain is making me crazy, and I'm desperately afraid my children will be hurt by it. I cannot do this anymore," I sobbed.

The Lord, my Refuge, met me once again. Like the joy and lightness I had experienced as a child inviting him in for the first time, he once more led me to green pastures and still waters to restore my soul. Those waters have—and still continue—to bring healing redemption. It's a divine exchange to daily choose to forgive and to replace the lies of the enemy with the truth that God declares over me.

The Lord sings over me and my responsive song is heard in the night. I am my Beloved's and he is mine. In that secret place, his perfect love is bringing freedom, and I cannot keep silent.

"Open your mouth for the mute, for the rights of all who are destitute, open your mouth ... defend the rights of the poor and needy."—Proverbs 31:8–9

Chapter 2

Bible Study

By Paige Henderson

Let's Start with a Cup o' Truth

I heard a Christian counselor say that we only have two emotions: fear and love. That's some power there! If you only have two basic emotions, then it shouldn't be too hard to control them, right? (I laughed as I typed that!)

As much as we try to control fear in our lives, often it can feel like the exact opposite is happening: fear is controlling us. Consider what Kim said about her fear of failing to live up to expectations: "The internal need to be the perfect Christian, wife, mother, daughter, servant, and businesswoman was crushing me."

Fear is crushing. What kind of fear is crushing you right now? Fear of people looking down on you? Fear of embarrassment? Fear of life unraveling? Fear of God's punishment?

Whatever the fear, there's something far more powerful than that fear—it's love, that is, God's love in and for us. Scripture tells us precisely what love does to fear: "There is no fear in love. But *perfect love drives out fear*, because fear involves punishment" (1 John 4:18; italics added). The apostle John also says in this passage, "God is love, and the one who abides in love abides in God, and God abides in him. By this, love is perfected with us, so that we may have confidence in the day of judgment" (verses 16–17).

Did you catch that? *Confidence.* That's courage, assurance, boldness, *not* being afraid. It is because of God's powerful love that we do not need to fear punishment. That's what this study is about: moving from life-crushing fear to life-freeing courage. The more that we allow ourselves to abide in God's love, the more that fear is driven out making room for courage to come in.

Let's start with getting a better understanding of the role fear plays in our lives.

The Worship Gene

God put a worship gene into your spiritual DNA when he made you. When God called out the purpose that he'd put into Adam to "tend" the garden in Genesis 2:15, he was calling him to worship. The word for "tend" in Hebrew means both "to work" and "to worship." You truly do work and worship. When you worship something you work at it: you revere it, you honor it, you learn more about it, you practice it, and you derive pleasure and identity from it. You protect it and defend it and justify your actions in worshiping it. You were given a natural inclination to worship and if God isn't what you're worshiping, it will be something or someone else: your career, your hobby, your first love, your abuse, your sin, your image, yourself. You were made to worship and to tend to the object of your worship.

The idea of worship is lovely and right when the object of that worship is God, isn't it? God is love and his love is the driving force behind our worship. Take love out of the discussion and you're left with the other basic emotion: fear.

What does it look like when fear is determining worship? Fear is an uncomfortable emotion designed to get you to move away from perceived danger and toward safety. Just as powerfully as love draws you toward the object of your love, fear pushes you away.

If you fear failure as a threat to your emotional safety and well-being, you will respond to that fear by running away from failure as far as you can and to a place of safety. So you cling to success. The stronger the fear of failure, the more compulsive the need to succeed. Success then becomes the object of your worship, driven by the force of fear. You revere success, you honor it, you learn all you can about it, you practice it at all costs, and you derive pleasure and identity from it because it has saved you from your fear. Consider the worship that would derive from a fear of rejection. You would escape to acceptance. Or if you fear injustice, you would perhaps run to control. See?

"But wait!" you might be thinking right now, "Doesn't the Bible say we should have the *fear* of the Lord?!" I'm glad you asked. There are two kinds of fear: (1) the fear of the Lord, and (2) the fear of everything else. Let's wade into those ideas and see how the object of your worship makes all the difference.

The Fear of the Lord

So what is this "fear of the Lord" in the Bible? The Hebrew word *yare'* means "to fear, to revere, to cause to frighten; to be or make afraid, to hold in reverence."

The fear of the Lord doesn't mean being afraid. If it were about being afraid, then our fundamental fear response would kick in and we would run away from the Lord seeking a place of safety, which would be out of his presence. Certainly being out of the presence of God is *not* a place of safety, so the intention cannot be for us to be scared. We don't fear the Lord because of what might happen if we don't, or what we might get as a reward.

The fear of the Lord is based on a deep understanding of who he is, what he can do and who you are before him. When you fully comprehend how powerful he is, how merciful he is when he doesn't have to be, how unexplainable his ways are and that he loves you deeply and tenderly, the awe of him will feel very much like fear and you will be captivated by him. This sounds very much like love, doesn't it? Perhaps love and fear are inseparable when it comes to the Lord.

Compare this idea of fear and love to the relationship that a feudal lord back in the medieval days would have had with the people who lived on his land. Everything is his: the land, the castle, the streets, the houses that surround the castle, the raw materials needed to survive—everything. You live on the lord's land because of his good graces.

You honor him because he owns your house. You respect him because it is his victory in battle that allows you to live in a house on his land in peace. You bless him because he allows you provide for your family and make a little profit on the side from the produce that you grow on his land. You don't want to offend him because the same sword that was victorious in winning the land can turn on you.

You aren't afraid of him, but you recognize his place of headship and your place of submission and reverence. When the harvest is bountiful, you thank the lord and celebrate. When the harvest is not so good, you celebrate that you have a place on his land to try again next year. When enemies approach, you run to the castle and depend on the great courage and battle skills of the lord to protect you. When the lord walks down the street you stare in awe at this great man who gives you everything you need, but whom you could never be. That's the fear that's in the Bible, but coupled with the One who makes that fear healthy and profitable: the Lord of Lords.

Here's another aspect of fear. God is the Maker of heaven and earth, right? Right. There are telescopes up in space taking pictures of objects so far away that you couldn't fly there in your lifetime. Seriously! If you were to get in a spaceship that could take you across space, you would board that ship and years later your great-grandchildren would get off! And that's flying as fast as we know how to fly! The distance is almost immeasurable; it works on a calculator, but it doesn't calculate in our experience. God says of himself in Isaiah 40:22 that the universe that we can't measure or travel across, the universe that we've not found the edge of yet, is like a curtain or a canopy compared to him. He is bigger than the universe we can't measure! The great mystery of the universe is like the canopy top of his bed—you know, if he had a bed!

That's awesome. That's the fear of the Lord.

Now that we are on common ground regarding the fear of the Lord, look at how it benefits you. Read the following verses, write them down, and circle within the verses what the fear of the Lord gets you.

Psalm 85:9

_____

_____

_____

Psalm 112:1

_____

_____

_____

_____

_____

Psalm 145:19

_____

_____

_____

_____

_____

Proverbs 10:27

_____

_____

_____

_____

Proverbs 14:26–27

_____

_____

_____

_____

_____

In the space below make a list of those words
and phrases that you circled in the verses above.

_____

_____

_____

_____

_____

_____

_____

Not a bad list at all, is it? Can you begin to set your heart and mind toward receiving these things? Which ones do you see are missing in you? Which ones would you say you would like to receive first? Ask the Lord. Spend some time in prayer right now and ask him to help you.

And Then There's the Fear of Everything Else

Other words for fear in the Bible are defined like this: dread, terror, fright, scare, anxiety, heaviness, horror, trembling, shaking. The objects of these fears and the outcomes to those who are fearful are significantly different from the outcome of fearing the Lord. The fear of everything else robs you of action. It steals your voice and it distorts the truth of God.

From Kim's Story

"Fingers of fear began to tighten around my throat."

In abusive situations, fear is the glue that holds the entire circumstance together. They are afraid you'll tell and they'll be punished. You are afraid to be punished, so you don't tell. They are afraid that you'll stop doing what they want you to do. You are afraid they'll expect you to do more. They are afraid they'll get caught. You are afraid they won't. They are the terrorists and you are the terrorized. The weapon is threats and harassment, spoken and unspoken, silent bullets fired at your soul. There is an invisible chain that curls around your ankle. Fear takes another hostage.

Let's see what the fear of everything else leads you to do.

Read Genesis 3:1–10. Now focus in on verse 10 and break it into chunks of understanding.

What ignited Adam's fear? What did he hear that made him afraid?

_____

_____

_____

_____

_____

_____

What did Adam do out of fear?

_____

_____

_____

_____

_____

_____

_____

Okay, **read 1 Kings 19:1–3**. The background of this story is that the Lord's prophet, Elijah, has just been victorious against the prophets of Baal in a showdown with fire. Because the prophets of Baal were found to be false, and false prophets were killed, these idol-worshiping prophets were put to death. It just so happened that Jezebel, the queen of Israel at the time, was a follower of Baal. That's the story leading up to these verses, just so you know!

What ignited Elijah's fear?

_____

_____

_____

_____

_____

_____

_____

What did Elijah do because of fear?

_____

_____

_____

_____

_____

_____

_____

_____

_____

Do you see a common response to being afraid in both of these stories? Run and hide. The fear of the Lord yields all that good stuff that you discovered in those verses. The fear of everything else results in running and hiding.

Jesus Defends Children

You need to know that children aren't supposed to be in the position of having to tell an adult "no" when it comes to abuse. Adults aren't supposed to abuse children. If you are the survivor of any traumatic childhood abuse and you carry the guilt and condemnation of what you should have said but didn't, or what you should have done but didn't, you need to know that you weren't supposed to be put in that position. The one held accountable is *not* you.

From Kim's Story

"I could not tell an adult 'no.'"

But the shame that is laid on you is as palpable as a thick, wet, woolen blanket. Victims of another's sin are not guilty of the same sin and perversion. If you were to be robbed by someone, are you guilty of the theft? No, you are the victim of their sin, and as the victim you're not guilty of their crime. In a similar way, you were affected by the sin of child abuse, you felt it and lived it, but you are not the guilty party. You were the one robbed.

Jesus addresses the terrorizing of children. If you are reading this and you were the victim of any abuse in your childhood, you may be surprised to know that. Although Jesus doesn't list all the abuses that you may have endured—in fact, he doesn't really list them at all—what he is talking about is very clear.

Read Matthew 18:1–6.

When Jesus is asked who the greatest in the kingdom of heaven is, what is his answer?

Why do you think he answered this way? What could he be referring to when he held up the humility of a child as his prime example?

_____

_____

_____

_____

_____

_____

_____

_____

Then at the end of his answer to the original question, comes a comment from him that wasn't asked for, but one he felt compelled to give regarding the abuse of children: "Whoever causes one of these little ones who believe in Me to stumble, it would be better for him to have a heavy millstone hung around his neck, and to be drowned in the depth of the sea."

To completely understand the abuse that has made Jesus so vivid in his word choice, you have to understand the word "stumble." The Greek word for "stumble" is *scandalizo* which comes from *scandalon*. Can you see the word "scandal" in there? That means nothing good is involved in this "stumble." The root of the word "stumble" is actually a noun, not a verb. It is the stick that is used in a deadfall trap. A deadfall trap works like this: a rock or something else heavy is propped up by a stick with a string attached to it. When the critter you want to catch steps under that rock, the stick is pulled and the rock crashes down on top of them and they are trapped—or squished. When Jesus talks of a little one being caused to stumble, he means that they have been entrapped, tripped up, enticed into sin, or made to offend.

Ask yourself...

- Do you see any choice in this word "stumble"?

- Do you hear any condemnation for this "little one"?

- Is there any judgment about what the "little one" was made to do?

Stop right now. If you are the "little one" in this scenario, how do you feel reading this? Record your thoughts.

_____

_____

_____

_____

_____

_____

_____

_____

_____

_____

_____

_____

Have you ever thought that Jesus was angry over what happened to you? What does Jesus say should happen to your abuser? (Verse 6)

_____

_____

_____

_____

Jesus was not ever careless with his words. Every word was purposeful and guided by the Holy Spirit. The little one was made to sin; she didn't trip because she is clumsy or fall because she was bad. She was pushed.

And Jesus is mad.

The sin isn't in the heart of the child to commit, but the abuser makes them. You didn't want to do whatever you were made to do or receive what you were forced to receive, but your abuser entrapped you, tripped you, enticed you into it with pretty words or terrorizing threats.

Jesus believes you because he knows the truth. He believes you because he knows the contents of all hearts. He reads the heart like a script. Words are not necessary when you deal in spiritual things. The heart is laid bare before the One who made it. So in every situation he knows who's to blame and who's blameless. That should be a source of great comfort for you.

Yet the feelings of shame or guilt that begin in childhood can be difficult things to shake free of. When a young child is traumatized and not given any comfort or helped to understand the circumstances, she is left to define that trauma using only her experience at the time. That's not enough experience to allow her to fully understand what happened. Once she has defined the situation for herself, the memory of the trauma and her childlike understanding of what happened are locked into her mind. If no other truth is offered to her, she will move into adulthood with an incomplete understanding.

Children can draw incorrect conclusions about the "why's" of what happened: *My dad left my mom because I got a C in spelling. My brother died in a car accident because I forgot to call him. Our house burned down because I yelled at my sister. My grandfather died because I didn't want to go see him when he was sick.*

In the statements above, can you see what the underlying "cause" of everything is thought to be? *This happened because I'm bad.*

We act out of what we believe. False belief is sown all the way to the foundation, and the building is in constant danger of destruction. The doorway is opened from the moment of this early childhood trauma to a lifetime filled with the fear of everything else.

Doing the Approval Hustle

Did you catch this statement in Kim's story? *"The need for approval became an idol in my life."* Can you relate to that in your own struggle to overcome fear?

From Kim's Story

"The need for approval became an idol in my life."

In the heart of one who has been rejected and hurt, there's a fear that's deeper than just not "fitting in." Value that hasn't been established in a healthy way ravenously stalks validation from any source. Rejection and hurt leave a fear that you'll never be accepted and healed. The issues come when you look for that missing value from other people instead of from God.

The seventeenth-century philosopher Blaise Pascal is quoted as saying, "There is a God shaped vacuum in the heart of every man which cannot be filled by any created thing, but only by God, the Creator, made known through Jesus." The piece that fills the vacuum is as unique and expansive as God himself. Because it's a piece shaped like God, any other piece won't fit, no matter how hard you push. You've put together a jigsaw puzzle, right? No matter how deeply you are convinced that the piece with the blue eye and the little bit of blue beach towel on the side goes into the last empty space of the puzzle, it just won't if it's the wrong piece. Pushing harder, forcing it, even yelling, won't complete the picture. It is frustrating and disappointing that the piece won't fit, but it won't.

Dave Busby said that sometimes we "do the dance to get the hug." What he was talking about is the crazy world of people-pleasing that's so easy to get swept away in when you are convinced that your performances and conciliations are the only way to feel accepted and approved. The "dance" is your particular version of performance for the audience of people that you consider the source of validation. The "hug" is the acceptance of those people, the Validators, who scoop you up in their big loving arms of accolades and applause for a job well done, successfully accomplished, perfectly performed. In that applause, the fear of rejection and hurt is deflected.

But approval shopping is a trap. There's a hole in your bucket, and as soon as the Validators fill it with their approval, it all drains out to reveal the scum of fear clinging to the bottom. What is that fear? You fear their rejection. You fear the punishment that might come when you don't do the dance right and they reject you because of it. And then the icing on top is the fear of not getting what you want, which is approval and validation. Wrap those fears together and you have a big ol' package called *the fear of man*.

Let's dive into the Bible and see what the Lord has to say about the fear of man and the healing of a hurt and rejected heart. Following is a series of verses that trace the unhealthy path of the fear of man. Read them, in some cases write them, and answer a couple of questions on each. Really think through what the verses are saying to you in your current situation.

The best way to begin to see that the truth of the Bible is as vital and modern as it ever was is to interact with it, talk to the Lord and be ready to receive customized revelation. Expect that these words will be living and active and written just for you today. Insert your own name in the verse; put in your current situation so that the Lord's words can be life and breath for you.

Here we go!

Write **Proverbs 29:25** in the space below.

_____

_____

_____

_____

_____

_____

_____

_____

_____

What do you think of when you think of a
snare or a trap? Why would someone use a
snare or a trap?

_____

_____

_____

_____

_____

_____

The second half of this verse is like the antidote for the fear of man. What is it?

_____

_____

_____

_____

_____

_____

_____

Read what Solomon, the wisest man ever, said in **Ecclesiastes 4:4**. "I have seen that every labor and every skill which is done is the result of rivalry between a man and his neighbor. This too is vanity and striving after wind."

Labor means "anything that wearies or worries." That reflects the idea of wearing yourself out doing the dance because you're worried that you won't get the hug.

The second word *skill* means "an action, either good or bad." Well that pretty much covers everything that your life consists of, doesn't it? You do "action, either good or bad" all day long.

Replace the words *labor* and *skill* with the ideas given to you above:

"I have seen that every_____ and every _____that is done is the result of rivalry between a man and his neighbor."

How many labors has Solomon observed that are vain efforts?

_____

_____

_____

How many skills has Solomon observed that are vain efforts?

_____

_____

_____

_____

_____

Why do we engage in these labors and skills?
What's the result? You may write your own
response, or use what Solomon says in this verse.

_____

_____

_____

_____

_____

_____

_____

_____

_____

What is the Lord saying to you about doing the dance to get the hug? Journal it below.

_____

_____

_____

_____

_____

_____

_____

_____

_____

_____

_____

_____

Let's look at **John 12:42–43**: "Many even of the authorities believed in him, but for fear of the Pharisees they did not confess it, so that they would not be put out of the synagogue; for they loved the glory that comes from man more than the glory that comes from God." (ESV)

How many believed in Jesus?

_____

_____

_____

Why didn't these new followers confess their belief in Jesus? Whom did they fear and what did they fear would happen?

_____

_____

_____

_____

_____

Keep in mind that the synagogue was the center of everything. It's where everybody hung out, where all of life took place. The synagogue was the center of approval.

What did they love more?

_____

_____

_____

_____

_____

The followers of Jesus who saw him in the flesh apparently struggled with the Validators, too, so the idea isn't new. Can you relate to this verse? Do you feel what those new followers of Jesus were feeling? Be honest and respond below.

_____

_____

_____

_____

_____

_____

_____

_____

_____

_____

_____

_____

_____

Consider these words of Paul in **Galatians 1:10:** "For am I now seeking the approval of man, or of God? Or am I trying to please man? If I were still trying to please man, I would not be a servant of Christ." (ESV)

When you make Jesus Christ your source of approval, you will find out that what God wants and expects from you is entirely different from what people want and expect. His goals for you and his measure of you is not only the opposite of what you think you're supposed to be doing, his measure is completely and utterly revolutionizing. And unbelievably simple! When you embrace that his will and opinions matter more than even your own, *then* your life will change.

"Love Conquers All" Was God's Idea First

Something as pervasive as the fear of everything else has to have a cure that is equally thorough. The answer for your fear is the presence and power of the Lord. Enough said. You don't need to hear this from me; you need to hear this from him.

From Kim's story

"[God's] perfect love is bringing freedom."

Read Psalm 91. Read it aloud and change "you" to "I," "me," and "my."

Make this personal. Declare it with your mouth. Open your mouth and use your voice. Even sing it if you like.

What was your favorite verse? Which one means the most to you? Journal it below.

_____

_____

_____

_____

_____

_____

_____

_____

Go to Psalm 118. Read the whole psalm and then we'll look at some particular verses. This is a Psalm (song) of thanksgiving to the Lord written by King David.

Verse 4: "Oh let those who fear the Lord say, 'His lovingkindness is everlasting.'"

What do those who fear the Lord say about him?

_____

_____

_____

_____

Verse 5: "From my distress I called upon the Lord; The Lord answered me and set me in a large place."

What does the Lord do for you when you call upon him in your distress?

_____

_____

_____

_____

_____

Consider that the opposite of a "large place" would be a confining place. What are some places that are confining? List a few.

_____

_____

_____

_____

_____

Think about the fear of man and of the situations that you have been through that have left an opening for the fear of man to reign in your heart. What are some of those confining places?

_____

_____

_____

_____

When the Lord puts you in a "large place," what do you think he is he doing in your life?

_____

_____

_____

_____

_____

Verse 6: "The Lord is for me; I will not fear; What can man do to me?"

What does being "for" something mean? Who were you "for" in the last election? What does that mean you did? When you go to a sporting event or watch one on TV, who are you "for"? What does that mean you do?

Consider that God is *for* you. What does that mean he does?

_____

_____

_____

_____

_____

_____

_____

_____

Can you receive this truth for you?

_____

_____

_____

_____

_____

Verses 8–9: "It is better to take refuge in the Lord than to trust in man. It is better to take refuge in the Lord than to trust in princes."

The phrase "take refuge" means to hurry up and run for protection. What is the difference in a man and a prince?

_____

_____

_____

_____

_____

_____

God is covering the gamut here, from just plain old ordinary people to people of prominence and influence who could actually promote you and give you status.

Verses 10–12: "All nations surrounded me; In the name of the Lord I will surely cut them off.... They surrounded me like bees; They were extinguished as a fire of thorns."

"They" is the nations that were giving David trouble. On any given day of David's reign someone from some nation was attacking some part of Israel. Read the verses again and replace "nation" and "they/them" with "fears."

How are all the people you are trying to keep happy and pleased with you like a swarm of bees?

_____

_____

_____

_____

_____

What will you do in the name of the Lord?

_____

_____

_____

_____

_____

_____

Verse 13: "You pushed me violently so that I was falling, but the Lord helped me."

Can you see the person or people who pushed you violently? Put their name in place of the general "you" at the beginning of this verse.

What happened when they pushed?

_____

_____

_____

_____

_____

_____

_____

What is your favorite verse of all these? Which one "speaks" to you where you are right now? If the next assignment were to write this verse on a card and tape it to your bathroom mirror,

which one would you choose? Write it in
the space.

_____

_____

_____

_____

_____

_____

Let's take a closer look at **1 John 4:16–18.**

Where is there no fear?

_____

_____

_____

_____

_____

_____

What casts out fear? Why?

_____

_____

_____

_____

_____

_____

_____

You're going to love this! The word *ballo* in the Greek means "to cast out, or throw out." What's more interesting is the idiom, or the common everyday use of this word. When the word was used in Greek, everyone knew you were throwing something out like trash or dung! *Dung*! That's what life-suffocating fear is.

Would it surprise you to know that, in this verse, the Greek word for "love" is *agape*? Agape love is unconditional love. Love with no expectations or requirements. Love that overcomes unmet expectations and disappointments. Love that sees your heart and knows your intentions even if the actions didn't quite measure up. Love that sees what was done to you and doesn't hold you responsible for it. Love that never quits, never loses hope, never withholds, and never fails.

Here's more vocabulary to increase the beauty of these verses! The idea of being "completed" means that the work hasn't been accomplished, yet. There's more to be done. You've really just begun, and the task or project isn't finished or the lesson hasn't fully been learned, yet. But don't quit! The completion is coming if you don't quit!

Now try a rewrite of verse 18. Make it yours. Substitute the ideas that we talked about for the actual words in the verse. Write it below.

_____

_____

_____

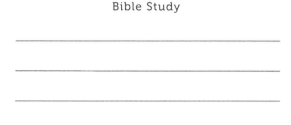

The only force powerful enough to cast out your fear of everything else is the presence of God. Love trumps fear every time. Why? The fear of everything else is perpetuated by our inability to "measure up." When there's no measure, you can finally rest.

Remember what was said in the beginning of this study? There are only two basic emotions that foster all the other emotions? Those emotions are fear and love. When fear dictates, love is silenced. When love reigns, fear gasps for air.

Oh, the verse-on-a-card thing? It's a good idea. (Wink)

Smart Girls Build on Rocks

So when you see the fear, smell the fear, and understand the fear, you do something about it. The only Fear Exterminator is God. But who takes care of all the little fear bug carcasses left on the floor? You do.

He can storm the gate and cast out the fear, but the clean up and the reinforcing of the gate is for you to do.

This is a part of tending to what you worship. Set the Lord squarely back on the altar of your heart, but then clean up the trash from the fear fest.

Read **Matthew 7:24–29** and explore what Jesus is saying to you today. Picture Jesus sitting next to you or across from you right now and hear him tell you this story.

The first set of people Jesus is talking about is the people who build on the rock. These people are those who do two things. What are those two things? (Verse 24)

They _____ the words of Jesus and they
_____ on them.

People who hear and act build where?

_____

_____

_____

Describe what you think of when you hear of
a house built on a rock.

_____

_____

_____

_____

What happened to his house when the super-
storm came?

_____

_____

_____

Now let's compare the people that Jesus describes at the beginning of verse 26. What two things do they do?

_____

_____

_____

_____

_____

They are compared to a man who builds his house where?

_____

_____

_____

_____

_____

Describe what you think of when you hear of a house built on sand.

_____

_____

_____

_____

_____

_____

What happens when the same super-storm comes?

_____

_____

The fear of man is like building your house on the sand. Jesus is the Rock, the foundation to your building.

Foundations are laid at the very beginning of a construction project. Everything else is built on top of that foundation. If the foundation is flawed or weak, then that building is doomed and it's just a matter of time before some outside force or inside pressure brings it tumbling to the ground. What kinds of things are in the foundation of your heart and mind?

It's in the foundation that you find those filters, beliefs, fears, pay-offs, motivations, inner vows, etc. that pervert and distort the nature and character of God and your relationship with him. These are the things that repel his truth, keeping it from going deep. Your filters and beliefs that are not based on his truth will continually thwart the healing and strengthening that he wants to do. They are revolution busters, and they ensure that *nothing* changes.

If these things are mixed with the sand of man, your house—your life—will constantly be shifting like coastline houses in Malibu. It doesn't matter how pretty they are or how much they cost or what famous people have dined in them, when the wind blows and the sand shifts, they slide into the ocean—castle and shack alike.

It's been my experience (I have relatives who live on the Gulf Coast) that people who don't take action when a hurricane is coming simply don't believe the word they've heard. They either deny that a hurricane is coming at all, or they don't believe the storm is as bad as the experts say it is, or they don't believe that their lives and possessions are in any danger.

We act on what we believe.

A Thought to Sip On

Do you believe that God is your source of help? Do you believe that he has not turned his face away from you? Do you believe that he is ready to give you all the validation you need because you are his? Do you believe that he is your biggest fan, cheering you on to fullness and joy? The abuse and fear have been false teachers to you and you learned a lesson that is a counterfeit to the love of Christ.

See how great a love the Father has lavished on you, that you should be called a child of God: and that is what you are (1 John 3:1). *That. Is. What. You. Are.*

Every good thing bestowed and every perfect gift is from above, coming down from the Father of lights, with whom there is no variation, or shifting shadow (James 1:17).

Every single thing that you are seeking to fill that emptiness left by rejection and hurt comes from the hand of God. He is your Source. He is your Applause. He is your Approval. All the good things and all the perfect gifts that you feel you have to be "good enough" to get have been yours all along. It may seem like they have been put on a shelf that's too high for your reach, stuck up there for the day you are "good enough," but God can reach them for you! He'll get them down for you, Precious, when you turn your eyes to him and ask. His gifts to you are not based on how well you do the dance. He doesn't tease you with phony promises like shifting shadow. He is the Father of lights—all light emanates from him. When all the light-blocking fears have been pushed out of the way, he will shine his light on what has been kept from you, so that you can see it, ask for it and receive it.

I don't know what translation you are using, but I am particularly fond of the King James

Version for Ephesians 1:6. It reads like this: "To the praise of the glory of his grace, wherein he hath made us accepted in the beloved."

Accepted in the Beloved, Jesus. Jesus is your hiding place, your place of refuge, your high tower, your hope, and your rescue. When you run into him you are safe. The bravest thing you can do is accept that you are accepted.

"Take Courage!"

In **John 16:33** Jesus tells his disciples, "These things I have spoken to you, so that in Me you may have peace. In the world you have tribulation, but take courage; I have overcome the world."

What can you expect in the world in which we live?

_____

_____

_____

How does courage come to you?

_____

_____

_____

Why can we be courageous?

_____

_____

_____

How would you define "courage"? No dictionaries or thesauruses or Google or Wikipedia, please! Just you and your own ideas.

Courage is …

_____

_____

_____

_____

I like to think of courage as walking into what you fear. If you fear losing your life, you have to walk at death with the intention of dying. Hunkering down to protect yourself in the war zone of life's experiences only results in the loss of life. Charging at the things that frighten you, releases you to really live. That just knocks reason completely off balance! But courage defies reason. Courage is, in its most essential form, unreasonable. When Jesus said to "take courage," he was inviting incongruence.

Jesus said to take courage like a bottle on the counter. "There it is," he says, "Take it." The next move is yours. He put it there, a bottle full for you to use, but you have to intentionally and with full understanding take it. Courage doesn't fall on you; you aren't seized by courage.

Tribulation happens. We live in a fallen world and the loop track in the background of life is a song of tribulation. Jesus has overcome, but you haven't, yet. You are overcoming. He has overcome, but now it's your move. Because he did, you can. These things that have hurt you, caused rejection, terrified you and scarred you are all overcome-able, but you have to reach out and take the courage that he left on the counter for you.

"When I am afraid,
I will put my trust in You.
In God, whose word I praise,
In God I have put my trust;
I shall not be afraid.
What can mere man do to me?"
—Psalm 56:3–4

Each of those in the "run and hide" examples we learned about earlier eventually chose to take courage. Adam and Eve settled outside of Eden and continued in obedience. It had to be a frightful thing to have walked with God, talked with God, tangibly felt him, and then to find him gone. But God had told them to be fruitful and multiply, and as far as we know they had produced more of themselves yet. They moved out of Eden and into their new place, but they did not stop in their obedience. They thrived in their new environment, growing crops and flocks and teaching their children to honor God. Cain and Abel and later Seth were born to them because they didn't continue running and hiding in fear. (See Genesis 4.)

Elijah pushed past his fear to continue to be a major guiding force in Israel after the deaths of Ahab and Jezebel, and he lived to see two more kings in Israel. He didn't cower away from the call of God even though it was that prophetic call that got him in trouble. He persevered to mentor Elisha and established him as the next prophet in Israel. Elijah was taken up to heaven in a whirlwind. (See 2 Kings 1–2.)

A Thought to Sip On

Have you ever had something go terribly wrong in your kitchen trash or in the refrigerator? You smell it and it's completely appalling and devastating to the otherwise peaceful environment. What do you do? Do you leave it and hope it just goes away or do you do something about it? You act on it, girl! You seize the offending bag and its contents or you rake the offending leftover into the bag, cinch it up (hoping you bought the leakproof, puncture-proof kind) and you throw it out.

There are no hazmat people to do that for you. You have to take it in hand and do something about it. That's the adventure of leaving fear behind, isn't it? The fear you've taken in must now be taken out like smelly trash. God's perfect love can do that for you, and you get to be a part of the process.

It takes courage to recognize that what you've filled your life with is the fear of man, not the fear of the Lord. It takes courage to recognize where you were caused to stumble and to receive, finally, that you are exempt from what you've been terrorized by. It takes courage to rebuild in a different location, admitting that what you built on before was sand. It takes courage to step right into what you are most frightened of to receive what the Lord most wants to give you: his peace.

"For I am the Lord your God,
who upholds your right hand,
Who says to you,
'Do not fear, I will help you.'"
—Isaiah 41:13

A Prayer

Lord, I am so thankful for all the gifts you have given me in my life. I know you are as much at work in my life as you are in the people that have brought pain into my life. Your grace, mercy, and love cover a multitude of sin.

Today, I confess you as Lord over my life. I want to follow you, not lead. I choose to forgive [list names of your offenders here] and ask that you would heal their brokenness. Help me to see what you love about them and transform my heart. I want to spread your fragrance and light everywhere I go. Consume my being completely with your love so that all fear is removed. Let my life radiate your life and love in me. Shine in me so that every person I come into contact with may feel your presence and healing power. May they see you in me. I pray for courage to take risks that cause me to confront my fears, for the sake of your name.

May my life be a living sacrifice that is true worship. Help me to love you and others with a radical, crazy love. Let your perfect love go deeper still in me to cast out all fear so that I am made whole in you. My bridegroom King, you have won my heart and I am yours.

Be glorified through your body and bride, here on the earth as it is in heaven. Let me say with confidence, I am my Beloved's and you are mine.

In Jesus' precious name, Amen.

Chapter 3

Steps to Freedom

By Sharon Kay Ball

Sexual and emotional abuse is a horrific way to destroy the core of a human being's soul and create fear and disempowerment in the individual. Abuse is trauma in a person's life.

The following steps are suggestions that will get you started on your healing journey. Give yourself permission to follow your heart without condemnation through this part of your journey.

As you begin your healing journey, you will meet grief and the many stages it brings to your process. It is important to know that grief is universal and it is different for each person. Generally these stages do not happen in the same order for everyone. As you move through grief, allow yourself to feel the movement, for when there is movement there is life, and where there is life there is *hope*. You will make it through, only to find yourself stronger. This is the gift of grief. It acknowledges how deep the loss is and then gives you strength to handle the depth of loss. Walk gently with yourself through these stages. Be kind, be still, and breathe. You will be amazed when you embrace your grief and no longer fear it. You will see it as your friend and not your enemy.

Recognize

Oftentimes, children of sexual and emotional abuse will not have anyone to help them process the abuse or the grief that follows. They learn to survive the abusive situation with coping mechanisms that work as a child, but eventually do not work as an adult. These children are more susceptible to "other" abusers in their adult life. Why? If they haven't processed the abuse as a child and understand their value and have a sense of self, they will minimize or not recognize future abusive acts as abusive.

It is okay to say you were a victim during that part of your life. In many ways you're like the victim of a drunk driver. Let's say a drunk driver came across the double yellow lines toward you and hit your car head on, leaving you paralyzed. Would you say to yourself, "I am not a victim. I could have prevented that drunk driver from crossing the line." No, of course not. You had nothing to do with the driver choosing to drink and drive. You had everything to do with being the victim in the situation. Remind yourself during this stage that the abuse was not your choice or fault. You were a child. Children do not choose to be abused.

The gift of hope and healing is yours to receive. Only you can accept it and give your life the option to recover. Remember you are like an injured person who can choose to go through physical therapy and have a quality of life, or choose not to. Remind yourself that moving from victim to survivor is a process—a vital one to your life. If you truly want to live again, you must choose to be a survivor and disempower the hold that the abuse has had over you.

Make the Decision

Make the decision to be a survivor. This commitment is a positive step in your journey. It acknowledges that you have been through a trauma and you have persevered. You will carry on despite the hardship. You will *live*. You choose to live.

Each journey is different, some find healing faster than others. Be careful not to compare your journey to another's. You are an individual, and your journey reflects your individuality.

1. Seek professional counseling to begin this part of your journey. Sexual abuse trauma is tedious and painful work. You will need professional support.

2. Create a "roundtable" team of supporters. These 2–3 individuals are your prayer warriors, your comforters, and your biggest cheerleaders for your recovery. They speak the truth in love and do not condemn you.

Remember and Believe

This part of your journey will be hard. It is very important that you be kind and gentle to yourself as you remember the traumas that were done to you. I would encourage you to meet with a qualified therapist to walk with you through these memories. These sessions will be hard, as they should be—trauma leaves deep wounds. You will need support during this time to allow yourself to feel the vulnerability that comes when you remember the hard stuff.

As children of abuse, God gives us many coping strategies to get through these hellish times. These strategies work during childhood. However as we enter adulthood we begin to see they do not work so well. The strategies of minimization or dismissing the memories become ineffective. You may find yourself having reoccurring nightmares of the abuse or intrusive thoughts or memories that you cannot control anymore. This is okay; you will be okay. These are imperative signals to you to replace the "old" ways with "new" ways of understanding your trauma.

It is important during this part of remembering, to believe yourself. Gently allow yourself to sit in the reality of the trauma that as a child you were not big enough to do. Children were not made to be able to handle these kinds of horrific things. I am so glad God gave children coping mechanisms to get through traumas like abuse. He allowed you to forget some of these horrific acts. Now as an adult, one of the greatest gifts is to *believe* yourself. Believe yourself for that little girl in you, that feared no one would believe you if you told. You are in a place now where you cannot be hurt again; you are an adult, and the little girl you once were needs to know you believe her.

1. Reconnect with the little girl inside. The little girl that suffered the trauma of abuse. Sometimes it is helpful to picture, if you have a child, your child going through such suffering. More than likely this image will bring you to tears, for you would never want anything like that to happen to your child.

2. Now, using that image of your child going through your abuse experience, what would you say to your child? What would you say to ease your child's pain? Would you comfort, would you hold, would you weep with your child? Or would you ignore, accuse or blame your child?

3. Write a letter to yourself as a child. Write a letter of what you feel you as a child lost as you experienced abuse. This is between you, her, and God.

4. Write a letter of hope for your future, acknowledging that the little girl in you will be terrified to trust and believe that anything good could happen. But you, now that you are safe and in recovery, will look out for her. She deserves to have a healthy, safe future!

Share

Secrets only carry power when they are kept secret! This may be a difficult step, but it is necessary to squelch the power of secrecy. With secrecy comes shame, and shame will hold you captive. This may take courage, but it could be a very empowering step for you to speak with someone about your story.

Anger

Anger is an emotion that God has given all human beings to let us know when something is wrong. It is a good emotion. During and after your abuse, you felt angry. This is good, very good. Now, how you guide your anger is what allows it to shape-shift and take on action. You have the power to use your anger in a positive way or negative way. Be very careful not to turn this anger inward—that would allow the abuse to then have power over you again. Explore healthy ways to use your anger—the righteous anger that God gave you to stand up against the wrong in this world. I would recommend the following ways in coming to terms with your anger.

- Journal about your anger, allowing your thoughts to form on paper. In doing this you might find that the root of your anger is sadness, which may redirect your anger toward mourning your loss. Remind yourself that these thoughts are only thoughts; they do not have power unless put into action. It is when you act upon your anger that you can hurt others. Sometimes just seeing your thoughts written down diffuses what power they might have had.

Should you become overwhelmed process, these journal entries with your counselor.

๖ Make a CD or playlist of your favorite, inspirational songs and listen to them when you feel the anger arise.

๖ Exercise. Take some of the energy that anger brings and run it off!

๖ Acknowledge your anger, don't stuff it. This anger is looking out for you. Anger is like an alert system, a warning sign that something is wrong. When anger is denied, it will sit within you and will surface in ways that you may not like. There is no way to get around anger. Allow yourself to move through it, trusting that God put that emotion in you to alert you to the "wrongs" in life.

Forgive

This part of your journey may be one of the most difficult, understandably. This part of your journey is very private, and for many women forgiveness happens on a daily basis.

- Forgiveness does not mean you forget the wrong committed against you.

- Forgiveness does not mean you are acknowledging that the wrong committed is now okay.

- Forgiveness does not mean you give up the righteous anger you have toward your offender.

- Forgiveness does not mean a renewal of the relationship with your offender.

Try writing a letter to your abuser. The first letter you write is for you only. For you to see the words that you would say to your abuser. Do not send it. Allow your heart to sit with the mixture of emotions that it brings up in you.

In counseling, ask if your counselor would sit and let you speak to her the words you would

like to say to your abuser. Explore the feelings
it brings up after you do this.

Engage God; share with him your reservations
and fears about forgiveness.

Your Spiritual Walk

It is important that through your recovery journey
you take notice of where Jesus is during the
process. Is he there beside you, weeping with you?
Has he left you? Is he condemning you? Does
he take on the emotion of the abuser? During
traumas we often find ourselves seeing Jesus
through the grid system of our abuse. This is
how Satan would want our spiritual walk to
continue. However, through the healing and
recovery process, you may begin to notice your
view of Jesus was skewed by the trauma and
that he now takes on a healthier role in your life.
Journaling will reveal amazing insights to the
progression of your spiritual walk during this time.

Making Peace, Moving Forward

The journey of recovery is long and hard. Be very kind and gentle to yourself. There will be days when you feel like you have gone one step forward and two steps back. You are in charge of your life; therefore, you are responsible for your self-care—no one else.

As healing occurs you may begin to notice behaviors you do that you no longer like or that no longer work for you. Be strong in letting those go. Acknowledge that they were behaviors and actions that may have kept you feeling safe and in control before, but they are not necessary to live life anymore. *Let them go.* You do not need them anymore, for you have done the hard process of picking up the shattered pieces and, with God's mercy, putting yourself back together again. So enjoy the freedom to make changes.

I often wonder if the last person a survivor needs to make peace with is not their abuser, but themselves. This may be true for you. For years you may have considered yourself your worst enemy, critic, and sometimes abuser. It is time to reconcile with yourself. When you can make peace with yourself, you can move forward. Moving forward may mean you are no longer in crisis mode, that you have found a balance to life.

It is also important to know that there is no end to the healing process. On this side of heaven, your heart will be in constant healing. Only when we are at Jesus' feet will we experience complete and total healing.